# The Hidden Project Management Code

Decoding the Real World of Projects
Beyond Frameworks and Tools

**PHILL AKINWALE, OPM3, PMP**

**PUBLISHER**
Praizion Media

COPYRIGHT © 2024

**The Hidden Project Management Code**

**Author**

Phill Akinwale, OPM3, PMP, ACP

**Published By:**

Praizion Media
P.O Box 22241, Mesa, AZ  85277
E-mail: info@praizion.com | www.praizion.com

**Notice of Copyright**

All rights reserved. No part of this publication may be reproduced, transmitted in any form or by any means including but not limited to electronic, recording, manual, mechanical, recording, photograph, photocopy, or stored in any retrieval system, without the prior written permission of the publisher.

**Printed in the United States of America**
**First Printing Edition, 2024**

All rights reserved. No part of this publication may be reproduced, transmitted in any form or by any means, including but not limited to electronic, recording, manual, mechanical, recording, photograph, photocopy, or stored in any retrieval system, without the prior written permission of the publisher. The author and publisher make no warranties or representation that use of this publication will result in success using AI or about the completeness and accuracy of the contents. The author and publisher accept no liability, losses or damages of any kind caused or alleged to be caused directly or indirectly by this publication.

## TABLE OF CONTENTS

INTRODUCTION TO THE HIDDEN PROJECT MANAGEMENT CODE ..................................................4

CHAPTER ONE: THE REALITY OF PROJECT MANAGEMENT ......................................................7

CHAPTER TWO: THE 80/20 RULE OF LEADERSHIP AND TECHNICALITY ...........................11

CHAPTER THREE: THE ART OF FACILITATION ......................................................16

CHAPTER FOUR: PROJECT MANAGEMENT AS AN INSPIRATION JOB ...............................21

CHAPTER FIVE: MOVING BEYOND FRAMEWORKS ......................................................26

CHAPTER SIX: REFLECTION ON THE HUMANS ......................................................31

THANK YOU FOR JOINING ME ON THIS JOURNEY ......................................................36

ABOUT THE AUTHOR ......................................................37

# INTRODUCTION TO THE HIDDEN PROJECT MANAGEMENT CODE

Project management is often portrayed as a meticulously structured and universally applicable discipline, packed with sophisticated tools, complex methodologies, and detailed frameworks. However, as I've journeyed across the globe, training and engaging with diverse organizations, a stark reality has emerged: **project management success is not about how much you know—it's about how relevant your knowledge is to the projects at hand.**

In every industry and company, the relevance of project management technicalities varies. Whether it's a pharmaceutical development project, a construction initiative, or a service-oriented task, the methods and tools that matter are tailored to the nature of the work and the goals of the organization. For instance, knowing everything about Earned Value Management (EVM) may be impressive, but it's meaningless in a context where such precision isn't needed. On the other hand, in fields like defense or nuclear energy, where every dollar and second counts, EVM can be indispensable.

This book was born from these insights—an accumulation of experiences and lessons from moving from company to company, industry to industry. Across these varied environments, I discovered a universal truth: **effective project management is about tailoring solutions to fit the unique needs of the organization and the project.**

**Common Threads in Project Management**

Despite the variations in approach, some principles remain constant—the **vanilla-flavored gospel truths** of project management:

- **Vision and Purpose:** Every project begins with a reason for being. Teams must understand not only what they're doing but why they're doing it.

- **Stakeholder Alignment:** Success depends on everyone being on the same page, aligned in their goals and understanding of the project's objectives.
- **Tailored Management:** The degree of formality and detail required varies. For some projects, like a nuclear plant shutdown, every task and risk must be meticulously documented. For others, like creating a new promotional campaign, a simple 10-item bullet list might suffice.
- **Team Inspiration:** A project manager must ignite the team's passion and purpose, fueling innovation and commitment.
- **Appropriate Monitoring:** Reporting should match the project's needs—some teams need tight oversight, while others thrive when trusted to self-manage.

These principles underscore the importance of recognizing that **project management isn't a one-size-fits-all discipline.** Instead, it's an art and a science that adapts to the project, the people, and the organization.

## Why This Book?

From the outside, project management appears grandiose—a parade of Gantt charts, sophisticated software, and endless meetings. But the real world tells a different story. Many projects are managed with simple tools like spreadsheets or even informal check-ins. Organizations often prioritize execution over methodology, focusing on results rather than processes.

For example, consider the stark contrast between managing the launch of a new consumer product versus shutting down a nuclear power plant. The former might thrive on creativity and quick iteration, while the latter demands precision, thorough documentation, and strict regulatory compliance. Both are projects, but their management styles are worlds apart.

Understanding these nuances is the essence of effective project management. It's about:

- **Tailoring your approach to the project's needs.**
- **Knowing when to use advanced tools and when a simple solution will suffice.**
- **Balancing technical skills with the ability to lead, inspire, and motivate a team.**

This book will break down the *hidden code* of project management—what truly drives success. We'll explore the reality behind the theory, the simplicity behind the complexity, and the leadership behind the technicalities.

**What to Expect**

In the chapters ahead, we'll dive deep into the foundational elements of project management:

- How to initiate projects with clarity and purpose.
- The art of tailoring plans to fit the team and the work.
- Inspiring teams to execute with passion and precision.
- Monitoring and reporting at the right level of detail.
- Testing and handing over deliverables with confidence.

Through real-world examples and insights, this book will help you strip away the myths and discover the true essence of project management. It will challenge you to rethink what success means—not just in terms of time and budget but in terms of team satisfaction, customer outcomes, and long-term impact.

Whether you're a seasoned project manager or just starting your journey, this book is your guide to navigating the ever-evolving landscape of project management with wisdom, adaptability, and purpose. Let's uncover *The Hidden Project Management Code*.

# CHAPTER ONE: THE REALITY OF PROJECT MANAGEMENT

When we talk about project management, the image that often comes to mind is a highly organized operation run on sophisticated software, with meticulous plans and precise execution. But as someone who has worked with and trained countless organizations across industries, I've learned that the reality is often much simpler—and more effective when stripped of unnecessary complexity.

## The Power of Simplicity in Action

One of the most illuminating experiences I had was as a founding member of the **John Maxwell Team**, a global community dedicated to leadership excellence. What struck me about this organization was the sheer volume of work we accomplished without being weighed down by elaborate tools or processes.

One of my mentors on the team, Paul, exemplified this simplicity. Paul managed enormous workloads, navigating contracts, partnerships, and deliverables with an ease that seemed almost superhuman. Yet, his methods were refreshingly straightforward. He didn't rely on massive Gantt charts or fancy project management software. Instead, it was **persistence, grit, and drive** that propelled him forward. To this day, I consider Paul one of the best program managers I've ever worked with—not because of the tools he used, but because of his ability to prioritize what mattered, communicate effectively, and deliver results.

## When Agile Outperformed the Traditional Method

A perfect example of simplicity triumphing over complexity came during a project with an **oil and gas organization**. Our task was to develop a learning system. Initially, we followed a traditional predictive approach, crafting detailed organizational charts and schedules. However, it quickly became clear that this method was slowing us down.

The solution? We pivoted to an **incremental Agile approach**. By focusing on delivering a **minimum viable product (MVP)** and fostering collaboration among stakeholders, we achieved results faster and more effectively. Delivering incrementally allowed us to adapt to feedback, adjust our priorities, and keep the project aligned with the organization's goals—all without the burden of rigid frameworks.

This experience taught me that the key to success isn't about following one methodology over another—it's about **choosing the right approach for the context and adapting as needed.**

**Lessons from Diverse Industries**

Working across industries has further deepened my understanding of how project management varies and what truly drives success.

- **Construction and Engineering:** These organizations often thrive on heavy technical tools like **Primavera**, risk registers, and complex scheduling software. The stakes in these industries—where human lives are frequently involved—demand precision and detailed planning.
- **Pharmaceuticals:** Surprisingly, in this highly regulated field, I've seen teams rely heavily on **Excel** and patchwork solutions to manage projects. While these methods often work, they can sometimes result in inefficiencies due to the lack of integration and over-reliance on manual processes.
- **Service-Based Organizations:** These teams often prioritize fast execution and customer satisfaction over elaborate documentation. The tools are usually simple—shared documents, checklists, and a focus on clear communication.

Despite these differences, a common theme emerges: **projects fail more often because of poor communication, lack of vision, and unaddressed risks than because of technical missteps.**

**The Vanilla-Flavored Truths of Project Management**

No matter the industry or methodology, certain principles remain universal. These truths form the backbone of effective project management:

1. **Have a Clear Vision and Purpose:** Without a clear understanding of *why* a project is being done, teams lose focus and motivation.
2. **Stakeholder Alignment is Key:** Ensure that everyone is on the same page from the beginning. Misaligned stakeholders are a recipe for conflict and rework.
3. **Tailor Your Approach:** Not every project needs the same level of complexity. A nuclear plant shutdown requires meticulous planning, while a marketing campaign might only need a 10-line schedule.
4. **Inspire Your Team:** A project manager is more than an organizer—they're a leader who ignites purpose, hope, and a sense of the greater good within their team.
5. **Monitor at the Right Level:** Over-monitoring stifles creativity; under-monitoring risks chaos. Finding the right balance is essential.

**The Reality of Execution**

When it comes to execution, what teams often need isn't more tools or processes—it's **ignition**:

- **Ignition of Purpose:** Teams perform best when they believe in the value of their work.
- **Ignition of Hope:** A motivated team with a clear path forward can overcome obstacles.
- **Ignition of the Greater Good:** When people see their contributions as part of something bigger, they innovate and push boundaries.

It's the project manager's job to provide this ignition, empowering teams to execute with energy and focus. At the same time, teams have a responsibility to ask questions and seek clarity, ensuring they're aligned with the project's goals.

**Monitoring, Control, and Handover**

Monitoring doesn't mean micromanaging. Think about the projects we manage in daily life: no one constantly checks in to remind us to meet personal deadlines. Similarly, in professional projects, trust your team to deliver—while providing just enough oversight to ensure accountability.

Finally, every project culminates in a handover. Regardless of the methodology, **testing and quality assurance** are non-negotiable. Thorough testing ensures the deliverable meets the required standards before it's handed over to the client or end-user.

**Closing Thoughts**

The reality of project management is far from the polished, tool-heavy picture often presented in training courses or textbooks. It's about understanding the unique needs of each project, tailoring your approach, and focusing on what truly matters: **people, purpose, and progress.**

As you move forward, remember that simplicity isn't a weakness—it's a strength. The best project managers don't rely on the fanciest tools or the most rigid methodologies. They succeed by connecting with their teams, aligning with their stakeholders, and adapting their methods to fit the project's context.

Welcome to the hidden code of project management. Let's uncover more truths in the chapters ahead.

# CHAPTER TWO: THE 80/20 RULE OF LEADERSHIP AND TECHNICALITY

In project management, there's a misconception that success hinges on mastering technical tools and frameworks. While these are valuable, they account for only 20% of what makes a project truly successful. The other 80%? Leadership. **Facilitation, emotional intelligence, and the ability to inspire and motivate a team are the real engines of progress.**

This chapter explores the importance of leadership in project management, focusing on how it drives team dynamics, resolves conflicts, and aligns people toward shared goals. Success doesn't come from processes alone—it comes from the conviction and influence of leaders.

**Leadership: The Cornerstone of Project Success**

At its core, leadership in project management is about creating conviction—the drive to do something meaningful and extraordinary. As one of my mentors once put it, *"Everything rises and falls on leadership."* Even technical excellence is driven by a leader's ability to inspire continuous improvement.

Imagine this: a technically brilliant engineer who lacks motivation may do enough to get by. But under the guidance of a leader who cultivates belief in the project's purpose, that same engineer can achieve far more. Leadership unlocks the human potential behind the tools and processes.

**The 80/20 Rule in Action**

Over the years, I've observed that while technical tools are helpful, they're not the deciding factor in most project outcomes. Here's why:

1. **Leadership Drives Team Alignment:**
    - When teams understand the *why* behind their work, they're more likely to stay motivated and engaged.
    - As John Maxwell aptly said, *"People buy into the leader before they buy into the vision."*
2. **Conflict Resolution is Leadership's Job:**
    - I've seen teams derailed by unresolved conflict. On one project, a colleague and I were constantly clashing, creating a toxic dynamic for the team. It wasn't until our leader intervened—literally handing us his credit card to go out and resolve our differences over lunch—that progress resumed. Great leaders understand that conflict is inevitable but must be managed to avoid becoming a stumbling block.
3. **Facilitation is the Secret Sauce:**
    - Leaders act as bridge-builders, transforming chaos into order and aligning diverse personalities toward a shared objective.
    - The best leaders aren't taskmasters; they're facilitators who guide discussions, foster collaboration, and ensure everyone's voice is heard.

**Psychological Safety: The Leader's Responsibility**

Psychological safety is a term often associated with Agile, but its principles are universal. Teams perform their best when they feel secure—when they know their ideas will be valued and their mistakes won't lead to blame. Leaders create this safety by:

- **Being Transparent:** Share information openly, even when it's difficult.

- **Demonstrating Empathy:** Understand and address the challenges team members face.
- **Encouraging Experimentation:** Allow room for trial and error, knowing that innovation often comes from failure.

As the Agile Manifesto reminds us, *"Individuals and interactions over processes and tools."* This philosophy underscores the leader's role in prioritizing people.

**Facilitation: The Art of Leadership**

Facilitation is more than managing tasks; it's about managing relationships, communication, and energy. Great facilitators:

1. **Turn Disruption into Opportunity:** Leaders with emotional intelligence can read the room, address tensions, and pivot when plans go awry.
2. **Encourage Collaboration:** Facilitation isn't about dictating solutions; it's about creating an environment where ideas flourish.
3. **Simplify the Complex:** One of my mentors on the John Maxwell Team, Paul, exemplified this. He managed large workloads with simple tools, focusing on persistence and clarity rather than overcomplicating processes. His facilitation skills allowed teams to work effectively without unnecessary overhead.

**Emotional Intelligence: A Non-Negotiable Skill**

Daniel Goleman's work on emotional intelligence highlights its critical role in leadership. Emotional intelligence involves:

- **Self-Awareness:** Recognizing your own emotional triggers and managing them effectively.
- **Empathy:** Understanding the perspectives and emotions of others.
- **Adaptability:** Adjusting your leadership style to meet the needs of the team.

Project managers with high emotional intelligence build trust, resolve conflicts, and inspire teams to achieve excellence.

**Real-World Examples of Leadership in Action**
1. **John Maxwell Team:**
    - On the Maxwell Team, I witnessed how strong leadership and facilitation enabled extraordinary results. Despite minimal tools, the focus on motivation and alignment ensured projects moved forward seamlessly.
2. **Oil and Gas Learning System:**
    - When shifting an oil and gas project to an Agile approach, the leader's ability to inspire collaboration and foster trust was the catalyst for success.
3. **Construction Projects:**
    - In construction, leaders who balance technical rigor with empathy and adaptability have consistently delivered results, even in high-pressure environments.

**Practical Steps to Strengthen Leadership**
1. **Resolve Conflict Quickly:**
    - Unresolved tension wastes time and energy. Address issues head-on, creating a safe space for dialogue.
2. **Prioritize People Over Processes:**
    - Tools and frameworks matter, but they're secondary to the people using them. Focus on building relationships and trust.
3. **Model Excellence:**
    - Set the standard by embodying commitment, integrity, and perseverance.
4. **Encourage Feedback:**

- Regularly ask your team for input on how to improve collaboration and leadership.

5. **Celebrate Success:**
    - Recognize and reward achievements, no matter how small. Acknowledgment fuels motivation.

**Closing Thoughts**

Leadership isn't just part of project management; it's the heart of it. The 80/20 rule teaches us that while technical skills are valuable, they are secondary to the human element. As you lead your projects, remember: success rises and falls on your ability to inspire, align, and empower your team.

In the next chapter, we'll explore how facilitation transforms chaos into order and equips leaders to navigate the complexities of project management. Stay tuned!

# CHAPTER THREE: THE ART OF FACILITATION

At its core, project management is about navigating complexity while bringing clarity and cohesion to a team. This is where facilitation becomes essential. A great facilitator is not merely a manager of tasks but a builder of bridges—between people, ideas, and processes. Facilitation transforms a disorganized, disparate team into a cohesive unit working toward shared goals.

This chapter dives into the essence of facilitation: how project managers act as orchestrators of collaboration, organizers of chaos, and champions of team dynamics.

## What is Facilitation in Project Management?

Facilitation is the art of making progress possible. It's about creating an environment where people can collaborate effectively, share ideas openly, and focus on achieving results. Unlike traditional management, facilitation emphasizes enabling rather than controlling. It's not about dictating tasks but about guiding the team to find solutions, align on objectives, and navigate challenges together.

Great facilitators:

- Help teams understand their goals and priorities.
- Ensure everyone's voice is heard, fostering inclusivity and collaboration.
- Remove obstacles that hinder progress, whether they're logistical, interpersonal, or process-related.

## Why Facilitation Matters

Facilitation is vital because project management isn't just about charts and schedules—it's about people. Teams are made up of diverse individuals with unique perspectives, motivations, and communication styles. Without facilitation, these differences can lead to misunderstandings, conflict, or stagnation. With it, teams can harness their diversity as a strength.

As I've seen across industries, the best project managers are also the best facilitators. Whether in construction, pharmaceuticals, or service-based organizations, facilitation has consistently proven to be the difference between a project that falters and one that thrives.

**The Facilitator as a Bridge-Builder**

One of the most important roles of a facilitator is bridging gaps—between people, processes, and priorities. Here are a few ways facilitators achieve this:

1. **Bridging Personalities:**
   - Teams are composed of individuals with varying working styles. For example, some team members may thrive on detailed plans, while others prefer big-picture discussions. A skilled facilitator identifies these differences and ensures that everyone can contribute in their preferred way.
2. **Bridging Communication Gaps:**
   - Miscommunication is one of the most common causes of project delays and conflicts. Facilitators ensure that messages are clear, consistent, and understood by all parties.
3. **Bridging Processes and People:**
   - Tools and frameworks can only go so far. A facilitator bridges the gap between rigid processes and the human element, adapting methods to fit the team's strengths and the project's needs.

**The Challenges of Facilitation**

Facilitation isn't without its challenges. A facilitator must often navigate:

- **Conflict:** Teams don't always get along, and unresolved conflicts can derail progress.
- **Resistance to Change:** Some team members may resist new processes or approaches.
- **Ambiguity:** In complex projects, it's easy for teams to lose focus or get bogged down in uncertainty.

These challenges require a facilitator to possess not only technical skills but also emotional intelligence, adaptability, and resilience.

**A Story of Conflict Turned Collaboration**

Let me share an example from my career that illustrates the power of facilitation. On one project, a colleague and I were constantly clashing—arguing over decisions, questioning each other's ideas, and creating a toxic environment for the rest of the team. The tension was palpable, and progress was grinding to a halt.

Our leader recognized the impact this conflict was having, and instead of ignoring it, he took action. He handed us his credit card and told us to go have lunch together and work things out. That simple act of facilitation—removing us from the workplace, creating a safe space for dialogue, and encouraging resolution—transformed our dynamic. We returned to the team more aligned, and the project moved forward with renewed energy. This experience taught me that facilitation isn't always about big gestures or formal processes. Sometimes, it's about small but meaningful interventions that allow people to find common ground.

## The Practical Skills of a Great Facilitator

What makes a great facilitator? Here are some essential skills:

1. **Active Listening:**
   - Facilitation starts with understanding. Listen not only to what is said but also to what isn't—nonverbal cues, hesitations, and underlying concerns.

2. **Empathy:**
   - Facilitation requires seeing the project through the eyes of each stakeholder and understanding their perspectives.

3. **Clear Communication:**
   - A facilitator must distill complex information into simple, actionable insights and ensure everyone understands the next steps.

4. **Conflict Resolution:**
   - As the example above shows, addressing conflict head-on and guiding people toward resolution is a key part of facilitation.

5. **Adaptability:**
   - No two projects are the same. A great facilitator adapts their approach to fit the team, the organization, and the specific challenges at hand.

## Facilitation Across Industries

Facilitation looks different depending on the context. Here are some examples:

1. **In Construction:**
   - In large-scale construction projects, facilitation often involves aligning multiple subcontractors, ensuring seamless communication, and managing dependencies.

2. **In Pharmaceuticals:**
   - Here, facilitation might involve navigating complex regulatory requirements while keeping the team focused on delivering results.

3. **In Service-Based Organizations:**
    - Facilitation is often about maintaining a customer-centric focus, ensuring that deliverables align with client expectations.

In each of these industries, the principles of facilitation remain the same: listen, align, adapt, and empower.

**The Leader as a Facilitator**

Facilitation isn't just a skill; it's a mindset. Leaders who embrace facilitation:
- Create environments where teams feel safe to innovate and experiment.
- Encourage collaboration and open dialogue.
- Remove obstacles, enabling their teams to focus on what matters most.

As John Maxwell says, *"A leader is one who knows the way, goes the way, and shows the way."* A leader who facilitates effectively doesn't just tell people what to do; they show them how to succeed.

**Closing Thoughts**

Facilitation is the art of turning potential into progress. It's about creating the conditions for collaboration, empowering teams to perform at their best, and navigating challenges with grace and empathy. In the chaotic world of project management, facilitation brings order, clarity, and momentum.

As we move to the next chapter, we'll explore how project management becomes a job of inspiration—connecting team efforts to a greater purpose and unlocking their full potential. Stay tuned.

# CHAPTER FOUR: PROJECT MANAGEMENT AS AN INSPIRATION JOB

Project management is more than timelines, budgets, and deliverables. At its heart, it is about inspiring people to do their best work and connecting their efforts to something greater than themselves. While methodologies and tools help keep things organized, it is the spark of inspiration that truly drives success. The best project managers don't just manage tasks—they ignite passion, align efforts with a shared purpose, and create environments where people feel motivated to excel.

The reality is that people don't come to work simply to follow instructions. They want to feel that their work matters, that their contributions are valued, and that they are part of something meaningful. This is why project management, at its core, is a job of inspiration. It is about creating belief—not just in the project but in the team's ability to succeed together.

## The Role of Purpose in Project Management

Purpose is the fuel of any successful project. When people understand the *why* behind their work, they are more likely to give their best effort. This isn't about lofty mission statements or abstract goals; it's about helping the team see the real impact of what they're doing. A marketing campaign isn't just about selling a product; it's about creating a connection with customers. A construction project isn't just about laying bricks; it's about building homes where families will create memories.

I remember working on a project where the team was overwhelmed by the sheer complexity of the tasks ahead. Progress was slow, and morale was low. Instead of focusing on the technical hurdles, the project leader called a meeting to remind everyone why the project mattered. They spoke not about deadlines or budgets but about the lives that would be improved once the project was complete. It was a simple yet powerful moment. Suddenly, the team had a renewed sense of purpose, and the energy in the room shifted. People who had been dragging their feet began stepping up, offering solutions, and working together with a shared sense of determination.

That's the power of purpose. It's not about manipulating people with grandiose speeches; it's about helping them see the real value of their work and how it contributes to something greater.

**Connecting Work to a Greater Cause**

Project managers often underestimate the power of linking individual tasks to a broader mission. In my experience, this connection is what transforms teams from a group of individuals into a cohesive, high-performing unit. People want to know that their efforts are making a difference. When you show them how their work contributes to the bigger picture, you unlock a level of commitment and innovation that no tool or process can achieve.

On one project, I worked with a team that seemed disengaged and disconnected. Each person was focused solely on their own piece of the puzzle, with little regard for how it fit into the larger goal. The project manager, noticing this fragmentation, began holding regular briefings where they shared updates on how the team's work was impacting the organization. They highlighted specific examples of how the project was creating value and celebrated individual contributions that made a difference. Slowly but surely, the team's mindset began to shift. They started collaborating more effectively, taking ownership of their work, and striving for excellence—not because they had to, but because they wanted to.

## The Emotional Connection to Success

Emotion plays a critical role in project success. People are not robots; they are driven by feelings, motivations, and aspirations. A project manager who understands this can tap into the emotional undercurrents of their team to inspire action.

This emotional connection is not about being overly sentimental or trying to force enthusiasm. It's about understanding what motivates each team member and creating an environment where those motivations can flourish. For some, it might be the satisfaction of solving a challenging problem. For others, it might be the opportunity to learn new skills or contribute to something meaningful. Whatever it is, a good project manager takes the time to uncover these motivations and align them with the goals of the project.

## Creating an Environment for Excellence

Excellence doesn't happen by accident. It requires a deliberate effort to create the right environment—one where people feel supported, empowered, and inspired to do their best work. This is where leadership comes into play. A project manager must set the tone for the team, modeling the behaviors and attitudes they want to see. This means approaching the work with passion and integrity, treating people with respect, and maintaining a relentless focus on the project's goals.

One of the most powerful tools in a project manager's arsenal is trust. When people trust their leader, they are more willing to take risks, share ideas, and go the extra mile. Trust is built through consistency, transparency, and a genuine commitment to the team's success. It's about showing that you care—not just about the project but about the people working on it.

Psychological safety is another critical component of a high-performing team. When people feel safe to speak up, make mistakes, and challenge the status quo, they are more likely to innovate and push boundaries. A project manager who fosters psychological safety creates a culture where people can thrive, even in the face of uncertainty and challenges.

**Inspiration in Action**

Inspiration isn't just about grand gestures or motivational speeches. It's about the small, everyday actions that show the team you believe in them and their ability to succeed. It's about taking the time to listen, offering encouragement when things get tough, and celebrating victories—big and small—along the way.

On one project, I worked with a leader who had a remarkable ability to inspire their team. Whenever we faced setbacks, they remained calm and focused, reminding us of the progress we had made and the impact we were working toward. They had a way of turning obstacles into opportunities, framing challenges as chances to grow and learn. Their optimism and resilience were contagious, and the team responded with renewed energy and commitment.

This leader understood that inspiration isn't about denying the difficulties of the work; it's about helping people see those difficulties as part of a meaningful journey. It's about creating a sense of hope and possibility, even in the most challenging moments.

**Closing Thoughts**

Project management, at its core, is a human endeavor. It's not just about tasks and timelines; it's about people—motivating them, supporting them, and inspiring them to do their best work. As a project manager, your most important job isn't managing processes; it's igniting passion, creating purpose, and fostering a culture of excellence.

As we move into the next chapter, we'll explore the practical tools and techniques that modern project managers can use to balance technicality with humanity, staying relevant in a rapidly changing world. But remember this: no tool or technique can replace the power of inspiration. It's the heartbeat of project management, and it's what turns plans into progress and dreams into reality.

# CHAPTER FIVE: MOVING BEYOND FRAMEWORKS

Frameworks are often the backbone of project management, providing structure, guidance, and a shared language for teams to operate within. Agile, Waterfall, PRINCE2—these methodologies offer a roadmap for navigating the complexities of delivering work. Yet, as I've seen time and again, frameworks can become a trap. The rigidity they impose can stifle creativity, alienate teams, and overshadow the very essence of project management: delivering value to people.

To truly master project management, we must learn to move beyond the frameworks. This doesn't mean abandoning them entirely. Rather, it means recognizing their limitations, customizing them to suit the context, and always keeping the focus on what matters most—people, purpose, and progress.

**The Framework Trap**

The promise of frameworks is alluring: a clear set of steps to follow, a system to keep everyone on track, and the reassurance that you're using "best practices." But in reality, frameworks are often applied without thought to the specific needs of the project, the team, or the organization. This blind adherence to methodology leads to inefficiencies, frustration, and even failure.

I've worked with teams that spent more time debating the nuances of Agile ceremonies than actually delivering work. I've seen organizations insist on using complex tools like Primavera for simple projects that could have been managed with a spreadsheet. In these cases, the framework became the focus, rather than the outcomes the framework was supposed to facilitate.

Frameworks are not a one-size-fits-all solution. A project to launch a new marketing campaign doesn't need the same rigor as shutting down a nuclear plant. Yet, I've often observed project managers applying the same rigid processes to vastly different scenarios. This is the framework trap: the belief that the methodology itself is the key to success, rather than the people and purpose behind it.

**Customization as the Key to Success**

The most effective project managers I've worked with have one thing in common: they adapt. They take the best parts of frameworks and tailor them to the unique needs of their project. This customization requires a deep understanding of the project's context—its goals, constraints, stakeholders, and team dynamics. It also demands the confidence to deviate from the prescribed path when necessary.

For example, on one project with an oil and gas company, we initially tried to follow a traditional predictive approach. We created detailed schedules, assigned resources, and developed a comprehensive project plan. But as the project unfolded, it became clear that the client's needs were evolving too quickly for this approach to work. Instead of clinging to the original plan, we pivoted to an Agile methodology, delivering incremental value and incorporating feedback along the way.

By customizing our approach, we not only met the client's needs but also built a stronger relationship based on trust and collaboration.

This willingness to adapt extends beyond methodologies. It's about simplifying processes, eliminating unnecessary steps, and focusing on what truly adds value. In many cases, this means using simple tools—like spreadsheets or shared documents—instead of investing in complex software that adds more friction than benefit. Simplicity is not a weakness; it's often the most efficient path to success.

**The Human Code**

At the heart of every successful project is a team of people, each with their own motivations, strengths, and challenges. To move beyond frameworks, project managers must understand and leverage the "human code"—the factors that truly drive people to perform at their best.

Motivation is a deeply personal and often underestimated force. People don't work hard simply because a framework tells them to. They do so because they feel connected to the project's purpose, supported by their peers, and valued by their leaders. Project managers who recognize this can create environments where teams thrive.

In one of my earlier roles, I worked under a leader who had an extraordinary ability to inspire. He didn't rely on rigid processes or elaborate tools. Instead, he focused on building relationships, understanding what mattered to each team member, and creating a sense of shared purpose. His approach wasn't about deliverables—it was about people. And the results were remarkable. Projects were completed ahead of schedule, teams felt empowered, and clients were consistently delighted.

This human-centric approach is what sets exceptional project managers apart. It's not about managing resources; it's about leading people. It's about bridging the gap between management and inspiration, turning individual efforts into collective success.

**Redefining Success**

Traditional measures of project success—delivering on time, within scope, and on budget—are important but incomplete. A project that meets these criteria but leaves the team burned out, the customer dissatisfied, or the organization no better off cannot truly be considered a success.

Real success is multidimensional. It's about fulfilling the project's purpose, whether that's solving a problem, meeting a need, or creating something new. It's about ensuring the team feels proud of their work and grows from the experience. It's about building trust and delivering value to stakeholders. And it's about aligning the project's outcomes with the organization's long-term goals.

I've worked on projects where the technical deliverables were flawless but the team was so exhausted by the end that they dreaded starting the next one. Conversely, I've seen projects where unexpected challenges forced delays, but the team emerged stronger, more cohesive, and more motivated because the project manager prioritized their well-being and growth.

Redefining success means looking beyond the immediate metrics and considering the broader impact of the project. Did the team grow? Did the customer's needs change, and were we able to adapt? Did the project leave the organization in a better place than before? These are the questions that matter.

**Creating a Legacy**

Ultimately, project management is about more than delivering results—it's about creating a legacy. The relationships you build, the trust you foster, and the inspiration you provide leave a lasting impact long after the project is complete. Great project managers are remembered not for the frameworks they followed but for the environments they created and the lives they touched.

Moving beyond frameworks is about embracing this larger vision of project management. It's about focusing on people over processes, outcomes over outputs, and meaning over metrics. It's about using frameworks as tools, not crutches, and leading with authenticity, empathy, and purpose.

**Closing Thoughts**

The framework trap is easy to fall into, but it's also easy to avoid when you prioritize what truly matters. Project management is not about rigid adherence to methodologies; it's about flexibility, customization, and understanding the human code. It's about redefining success to include fulfillment, growth, and alignment with greater goals.

As you continue your project management journey, remember this: frameworks are a starting point, not an endpoint. The true art of project management lies in knowing when to follow them, when to bend them, and when to leave them behind.

In the next chapter, we'll explore how project managers can create environments where people want to excel, diving deeper into the connection between leadership, motivation, and lasting success.

# CHAPTER SIX: REFLECTION ON THE HUMANS

Leadership, team dynamics, and emotional intelligence are the unseen forces behind every successful project. While tools and techniques have their place, they pale in comparison to the influence of effective leadership. At its core, project management is a human endeavor, and humans thrive—or stumble—based on the leadership that surrounds them.

## Why Leadership Matters

Project success doesn't just hinge on plans, schedules, or technical abilities; it hinges on the people involved and their ability to work together toward a shared goal. And at the heart of that collaboration lies leadership. Leadership creates the conviction and drive necessary to achieve excellence, even when technical skills fall short.

As John Maxwell aptly says, *"Everything rises and falls on leadership."* This truth reveals itself in every aspect of project management, from resolving conflicts to fostering innovation and aligning a team toward a common vision.

## The Reality of Team Dynamics

No team is immune to conflict. It's a natural byproduct of bringing together individuals with diverse personalities, goals, and working styles. However, unresolved conflict can quickly morph into a stumbling block that derails progress and morale.

I remember a vivid example of this during one of my projects. A colleague and I were caught in a constant cycle of conflict—what could only be described as a *"cat-and-dog scratching"* dynamic. The tension wasn't just affecting us; it was becoming an obstacle for the entire team. Eventually, my boss, frustrated with the impasse, handed us his credit card and told us to go have lunch together to resolve the issue. That simple act of leadership was transformative. By creating a space for open dialogue, we were able to move past our differences, restore cordiality, and refocus on the team's objectives.

**Leadership and Emotional Intelligence**

Great leaders understand that conflict, when managed effectively, can strengthen a team. This requires emotional intelligence—the ability to navigate interpersonal relationships with empathy, self-awareness, and tact. Emotional intelligence is not just a nice-to-have skill; it's the bedrock of leadership.

Daniel Goleman, a pioneer in the field of emotional intelligence, notes, *"What distinguishes great leaders from merely good ones isn't IQ or technical skills. It's emotional intelligence."* This means:

- Recognizing and addressing the emotions of team members.
- Being self-aware enough to regulate your own reactions.
- Creating an environment of psychological safety where people feel valued and secure.

When leaders foster psychological safety, as emphasized in the Agile Manifesto, they unlock the potential of their teams. People are more likely to take risks, innovate, and strive for excellence when they know their work environment is a safe space for ideas and collaboration.

**The Conviction to Inspire Excellence**

Leadership isn't just about getting tasks done; it's about inspiring others to do their best work. I've seen this firsthand in my own career. When a leader demonstrates conviction—an unwavering belief in the project's mission—it becomes infectious. Even the most technically skilled team members need inspiration to strive for excellence.

As a leader, you set the tone for the team. *"A leader is one who knows the way, goes the way, and shows the way,"* Maxwell reminds us. By modeling excellence, you cultivate it within your team. This is why leadership remains the constant variable in project success, no matter the tools or methodologies employed.

**Practical Lessons in Leadership**

From my experience, here are some key lessons for project managers seeking to lead effectively:

1. **Resolve Conflict Early:** Don't let unresolved tensions fester. Create opportunities for team members to address issues constructively, whether it's through a mediated discussion, a team-building exercise, or something as simple as a shared meal.
2. **Foster Psychological Safety:** Let your team know it's okay to take risks and make mistakes. This doesn't mean tolerating subpar performance, but it does mean encouraging a growth mindset.
3. **Focus on Communication:** A leader's ability to communicate openly, listen actively, and bridge divides is often the difference between a cohesive team and one in chaos.
4. **Set the Standard for Excellence:** Excellence starts at the top. If you demonstrate passion, commitment, and integrity, your team is more likely to follow suit.
5. **Empower, Don't Micromanage:** Trust your team to get the job done. Provide guidance and support, but resist the urge to control every detail.

**Inspiration in Action**

Leadership often requires creativity and resourcefulness. One of my mentors on the John Maxwell Team, Paul, exemplified this. Paul managed extraordinary workloads with simple tools, prioritizing clear communication and persistence over complexity. His leadership inspired those around him to take ownership and execute with precision.

Similarly, I've seen project managers in the oil and gas sector pivot to Agile approaches, embracing incremental delivery to foster collaboration and achieve rapid results. These leaders didn't rely on rigid frameworks; they relied on their ability to align teams around a common goal and adapt to changing circumstances.

**Closing Thoughts**

The truth is, even the most technical projects depend on the human element. A technically brilliant engineer or project manager can only excel when inspired by strong leadership. Leadership creates the environment where skills are honed, teams are unified, and goals are achieved. It's what transforms a group of individuals into a high-performing team.

As you lead your projects, remember: people don't care how much you know until they know how much you care. Build trust, foster collaboration, and inspire excellence. The tools and techniques will follow. This is the essence of leadership—and the key to unlocking your team's potential.

**Next Steps: Reflection and Action**
1. **Have you ever fallen into the "framework trap"?**
    - Reflect on a project where you adhered too rigidly to a methodology. How did it impact the team, the customer, or the outcomes? What could you have done differently?
2. **How adaptable are your current project management practices?**
    - Consider a recent project. Did you tailor your approach to the unique needs of the team and stakeholders, or did you rely on a standard framework?
3. **Are you prioritizing people over processes?**

- Think about the human dynamics in your projects. Are you fostering motivation, trust, and collaboration, or are you overly focused on tools and metrics?

4. **How do you define success?**
    - Beyond delivering on time and on budget, what metrics or indicators do you use to measure the broader impact of your projects? Are you considering team growth, customer satisfaction, and long-term value?

5. **What steps can you take to move beyond frameworks?**
    - Identify one area in your current approach where you could simplify processes, customize a methodology, or prioritize outcomes over procedures.

6. **Are you building a legacy as a project manager?**
    - Reflect on how your leadership style affects the people you work with. Are you creating environments where teams thrive and grow? What can you do to leave a lasting positive impact?

## THANK YOU FOR JOINING ME ON THIS JOURNEY

As we conclude this exploration of *The Hidden Project Management Code*, I want to thank you for walking alongside me through the pages of this book. Together, we've uncovered the deeper truths of project management—the realities behind the frameworks, the importance of leadership, and the power of human connection.

This journey wasn't just about delivering projects; it was about understanding people, embracing purpose, and redefining success. Whether you're a seasoned project manager or just beginning your path, my hope is that these insights will inspire you to approach your work with greater clarity, confidence, and compassion.

Remember, project management isn't just a job—it's a responsibility and an opportunity. It's the chance to lead with purpose, empower others, and leave a lasting legacy. The tools and techniques will always evolve, but the core principles—vision, trust, and inspiration—are timeless.

Thank you for allowing me to share my experiences, lessons, and reflections with you. The journey doesn't end here. It continues with every project you take on, every challenge you navigate, and every person you inspire. Here's to your ongoing success and to the extraordinary impact you'll make in the world of project management.

Let's keep building, together.

– Phill

# ABOUT THE AUTHOR

**Phill Akinwale, OPM3, PMP**

Phill C. Akinwale, PMP, stands as a distinguished project management professional with a rich history of accomplishments in both the public and private sectors. His extensive experience includes collaborations with esteemed organizations, training professionals globally, and contributing to the field through numerous certifications and publications. As a certified coach, speaker, and prolific author, Phill is dedicated to guiding individuals and organizations toward success in project management, leadership, and personal development.

Phill's expertise extends across a diverse range of industries including IT, Training, Aerospace, Engineering, Health, Gaming, and Multimedia. His strategic leadership in these projects reflects his ability to adapt and innovate in an evolving professional landscape. As a valued participant in the development of PMBOK® Guide's Fourth, Fifth, and Sixth editions, Phill has directly influenced the standards and practices of project management.

Beyond execution, Phill is an author, trainer, and coach, contributing to the continuous development of project management disciplines. His engagement with government agencies such as the FBI, USACE, US Army, NASA, DOT, DOC, and USAF as a trainer and coach demonstrates his dedication to elevating project management proficiency on a global scale.

A prolific author, Phill has authored numerous works aimed at guiding professionals in project management, leadership, and personal development. His certifications and published works are testament to his commitment to the advancement of the field.

Phill C. Akinwale, PMP, invites those who seek personalized advice, coaching, or additional insights to connect with him. Leveraging his extensive experience and certifications, Phill is a wellspring of knowledge, offering growth opportunities for both individuals and organizations. His contact information is available for those interested in coaching or venturing deeper into his comprehensive literary contributions.

For a deeper engagement with Phill C. Akinwale, PMP, or to learn more about his contributions to project management and leadership, reach out through the provided contact information. Phill is dedicated to sharing his wealth of knowledge and experience with those looking to elevate their professional journey in project management and beyond.

Connect with Phill C. Akinwale, PMP:

- Website: www.pmanonymous.com
- Coaching Services: 1-1 Assistance
- Books on Audible and Everywhere Books Are Sold
- Website: http://praizion.com
- YouTube Channel: @praizion
- Author Instagram: @projectmanagementcoach
- Twitter: @praizion

Note: Phill C. Akinwale, PMP, offers coaching services at www.pmanonymous.com and has authored over 30 books, available on Audible and major bookstores.

All the best in your journey of mastering interview dynamics and achieving professional excellence.

www.ingramcontent.com/pod-product-compliance
Lightning Source LLC
Chambersburg PA
CBHW082258220526
45469CB00009B/3055